scribble in front cover on issue 25/11/09

HOW THEY MADE THINGS WORK!
THE ROMANS

Written by Richard Platt • Illustrated by David Lawrence

W
FRANKLIN WATTS
LONDON•SYDNEY

First published in 2008 by Franklin Watts

Text copyright © Richard Platt 2008
Illustrations copyright © Franklin Watts 2008

Franklin Watts
338 Euston Road
London NW1 3BH

Franklin Watts Australia
Level 17/207 Kent Street
Sydney NSW 2000

A CIP catalogue record is available from the British Library.

Dewey number: 609

ISBN 978 0 7496 7479 3

Printed in China

Franklin Watts is a division of Hachette Children's Books,
an Hachette Livre UK company.

Editor in Chief John C. Miles
Art Director Jonathan Hair
Designers Rachel Hamdi and Holly Fulbrook
Picture research Sarah Smithies

Picture credits:
Andrea Krause, istockphoto: 17 (c). Bettmann, Corbis: 17 (bl). Brian
Hoffman, Alamy: 26. Christophe Boisvieux, Corbis: 9. Danilo
Ascione, istockphoto: 17 (tr). Eckhard Slawik, Science Photo Library:
16. Hervé Champollion, akg-images: 7. Jack Sullivan, Alamy: 23.
Jeremy Voisey, istockphoto: 12. Jupiter Images, Agence Images,
Alamy: 15. Larry Mulvehill, Science Photo Library: 19. Martin Child,
Digital Vision, Getty Images: 29. Peter Connolly, akg-images: 25.
Visual Arts Library (London), Alamy: 11.

Contents

HOW THE ROMANS MADE THINGS WORK

In the middle of Italy's boot-shaped land, modern Rome is a great, exciting, bustling capital city. Two thousand years ago, Rome was all these things – and much more. For Roman people ruled most of the known world. They used technology and invention to control, expand and strengthen their empire.

Ave!

Roads and war machines

Warfare had made Rome strong. Roman soldiers were fierce, brave and disciplined fighters. They also got some serious help in winning battles from military inventors. These engineers created war machines, both big and small, to hurl missiles at the enemy with deadly accuracy. Engineers also planned Rome's roads. This network of paved highways enabled the Empire's armies to march at speed, putting down rebellions and capturing new lands.

Comfortable, healthy cities

At home in Rome, technology had a more peaceful purpose. It filled the city with grand buildings, and made the lives of the wealthy pleasant and healthy. Roman builders perfected concrete, arches and domes. Keen to keep their city clean, Roman engineers piped in fresh water and built a simple sewer system. They even invented central heating to warm their public baths and later their houses.

Though few of their inventions were really new and original, Romans were expert at taking good ideas and improving them. Much of what they created still exists today – a lasting reminder of an ingenious people who valued comfort as much as conquest.

Say it in Latin!

There are phrases throughout this book in Latin, the language of the Romans. You can find out what they mean on page 31.

CONCRETE

Since ancient times, builders have glued stone blocks together with lime mortar. This powder, made by heating and crushing limestone, sets hard when mixed with water. But, in about 300 BCE, Roman engineers made an amazing discovery. They found that if they added the right kind of sand to the "glue" they could make walls without any stone blocks. Today the new material they invented — concrete — is part of every building.

Roma in una die non aedificata est.

Baffled builders

Rome was having a building boom, but constructing new buildings was slow and costly. Brick wasn't grand enough for government buildings, and stone such as marble had two disadvantages: it was hard to cut and carve, and required skilled masons to work it; and it was expensive. A new material was needed urgently.

Workers mixed the special sand with "slaked lime" cement, which they stored in pottery jars until they needed it.

To make the concrete strong they added just enough water to make a thick paste.

Stirring the concrete made sure that the sand, lime and water mixed thoroughly.

Sandy solution

When Roman builders making mortar mixed in sand from the town of Pozzuoli, the mixture set as hard as rock – even under water. The "sand" was actually ash from Vesuvius, a nearby volcano. It contained special chemicals that reacted with the lime.

The builders realised that they could pound the grey paste into moulds to shape whole walls. A thin layer of marble in front of the concrete disguised its dull grey surface.

To build a dome, Roman engineers first constructed a formwork of timber.

Rubble blocks set in wet concrete strengthened it.

Tamping concrete down

Mixing concrete in a trough

Concrete was packed over formwork.

Adding more concrete mixture

Removing the formwork revealed the finished structure.

The formwork which supported the dome was made of timber.

Aspdin improves

Nobody improved on Roman concrete until British bricklayer Joseph Aspdin (1778-1855) made what he called "Portland cement" in 1824.

Trajan's Market

Moulded concrete forms many of the arches of Trajan's Market, which was built in Rome around 110 CE. The walls of the shops on the ground floor walls were once decorated with mosaic tiles.

THE ARCH

Striding boldly across a valley on thick stone legs, a Roman bridge holds a water channel nearly 50 metres (160 feet) up in the air. Built entirely without cement, this extraordinary bridge still stands, some 2000 years after its construction. To make it possible, Roman engineers invented a new kind of structure: the arch.

Stupui videre te hic!

Weak stone

Stone is strong when squeezed, but breaks easily when stretched and bent. So stone slabs used in building had to be massive – and very short. In buildings where stone lintels (beams) held up walls and roofs, the doorways, rooms and windows were very small. Stone bridges spanned only narrow streams.

Force acts on stone lintel and cracks it.

Arch spreads load evenly so that supports take the strain.

Arch solution

Roman builders made arches from carefully shaped blocks. First, though, they made wooden frames called centring, to hold up the blocks during construction. Once the last block at the top, called the keystone, was in place, the arch supported itself. Then the centring could be removed.

Building an arch

The half-circle-shaped wooden centring holds up the blocks until the arch is complete.

Centring built over supporting pillars

Stones forming one-half of arch in place.

The Pont du Gard

The Pont du Gard is a bridge in southern France that carries an aqueduct (see pages 20-21) . It was built to bring water to the Roman city of Nîmes. Roman architects built the Pont du Gard with three rows of arches because the pillars supporting taller arches would have been too slim, and might have buckled and fallen. Triple arches could be made more solid.

The Pont du Gard, built by Roman engineers, still stands today.

Stones forming other half of arch in place.

Keystone pushing down at top of arch keeps it in place.

Completed arch

BOOKS WITH PAGES

The book you're reading is a miracle of Roman information technology! Look closely: each sheet of paper between the covers is cleverly hinged along one edge. You can flick through easily, and move instantly from the beginning to the end. Sounds obvious? So why didn't anybody think of it before Roman general Julius Caesar (100-44 BCE)?

Da mihi volumen, sis?

Skip to the end of the scroll

Before there were books as we know them, people read from scrolls (1). These were written by hand, across long strips of paper or animal skin. Rolling the strip up made it easy to store and carry. Reading it wasn't as easy, though. To go from the beginning to the end you had a lot of unrolling to do.

A general idea…

According to Roman legends, when Julius Caesar was conquering France around 50 BCE he folded up long scrolls he received from Rome into equal-sized zig-zag pages (2). Then people began to write across the zig-zags (3). The idea of sewing half the folds together and cutting the others, to make what we now call a codex (4), came later.

Christian codex

The codex was not very popular at first. It was used only for notes and accounts until the end of the first century CE. Early Christians helped the codex replace the scroll. They wrote their Bible (holy book) on a codex to make it look different from the scrolls that Jews used for their holy writings.

The Codex Sinaiticus is a 1700-year-old Bible. It was written when the Romans were still powerful.

Manuscript marvels

Today we call a book a codex when its pages are handwritten. Proper books began with the invention of printing in the 15th century.

Before Caesar, Romans already used books of a kind – but they had only two pages. They scribbled notes on wax-covered wooden tablets hinged along one edge.

New technology

The invention of the codex also introduced another idea we take for granted: writing in columns. Placed side-by-side, these narrow strips of words make reading easier. When you read to the bottom of one column, you start again at the top of the next one to the right.

SPECTACLE ENTERTAINMENT

A deafening roar fills the giant stadium. Fifty thousand people cheer the plucky sailors fighting a mock naval battle. Then the "ocean" drains away. Fierce jungle animals spring onto the sand, and another dramatic combat begins. It sounds just like a modern circus, but this show took place in Rome 1900 years ago.

Verbera eum!

Bloodthirsty Romans

Rome's rulers worried about their popularity. If the Roman people didn't like them, they might overthrow them. To please the people the emperors staged munera: fights to the death between gladiators (warrior slaves). However, nowhere in Rome was big enough to hold all the people who wanted to watch the shows.

A mymillo, with his fish-like helmet (left, takes on a retiarius armed with a trident and net.

Massive marvel

Roman emperor Vespasian (9–79 CE) ordered a vast new amphitheatre or stadium: the Colosseum. Much of it was built of concrete (see page 6), and 80 wide arches (see page 8) allowed the crowds to quickly fill the stadium — and leave just as fast when the show ended. The giant stadium had numbered seats and tickets, and huge, movable shades to keep the sun off the crowds. A nearby aqueduct supplied water to flood the arena.

Vespasian's amazing stadium still stands in the centre of Rome, though the statues that once stood in its 240 arches were removed long ago.

Masts around the outside held up the canvas sun shades, which sailors adjusted like the sails on a ship.

Spectator spew

The passageways leading out were called vomitoria. From this Latin word, meaning "to throw out quickly" we get vomit – the English word for being sick.

Seats were free, but showed a spectator's importance. VIPs sat at the front; women, slaves and the poor watched from the high back seats.

A spectator's tessera (ticket) showed their sector, row and seat.

A maze of underground rooms, added soon after the Colosseum was complete, contained stage lifts to launch wild beasts instantly into the arena.

13

WATER WHEELS

Grinding grain by hand is hard work: to mill enough flour for three loaves takes two hours. This didn't matter when war and conquest provided the Romans with prisoners to work as slaves in mills. But when the Empire weakened in the third century CE the supply of slaves dried up. Then bakers looked for a new source of power.

Medicam turbo!

Muscle mills

The Romans knew about water wheels, but preferred muscle-powered mills such as the one below when slaves were cheap. When the price of slaves rose, Roman engineers realized that existing millwheels did not work well. They needed a supply of fast-flowing water; and they turned too slowly, grinding enough grain for just one family.

At most bakers, pairs of slaves turned huge hour-glass shaped stones to grind flour.

Current affairs

When Germanic people attacked Rome in 537 CE, they broke the aqueducts supplying water to the mills. To avoid starvation, the general defending the city rebuilt the mills on barges. Moored on the River Tiber, the wheels turned in the current.

Wheely great idea

To make sure the water wheel would turn in slow-flowing Italian rivers, Roman engineers made it bigger, turned the wheel on its side, and fitted more paddles. But fixed upright in the mill, the wheel could not drive grindstones directly. So an ingenious Roman used simple peg-and-cage gears to make the power "go round a corner" and turn a pair of level millstones set above.

Water wheel

This improved wheel is called a "Vitruvian" water wheel, after the writer Vitruvius (c.80 BCE – 25 BCE) who first described it. People across Europe copied the Roman design, and by the Middle Ages most water mills worked like this.

Cage gears engage with pegs

Pegs on larger wheel

Sell those slaves!

A pair of grindstones powered by a water wheel could turn 15-20 kg of grain into flour every hour. This was twice or three times what a pair of slaves could produce using a hand mill.

French flour

None of the Roman water wheels have survived, but at Barbegal, France, you can still see the remains of a giant mill they powered (left). The 16 pairs of grindstones that turned here milled nearly 30 tonnes of flour a day: enough to make bread for 80,000 people. An aqueduct brought water to power the wheels.

CALENDAR

Da mihi vinum.

Romans called it the "Year of Confusion". Julius Caesar had changed the calendar so it matched the passing seasons. But to fix the problem, and to make sure that every following year was just the right length, 46 BCE had to have an extra 11 weeks. Yikes! It lasted a whopping 445 days.

Mixed-up months

Romans measured their months using the moon's phases. There are 28 days between each full moon, making a Roman year $12 \times 28 = 336$ days. Romans thought that $366 \frac{1}{4}$ days passed between one Midsummer day and the next. So to make the calendar match the seasons they added an extra month every eight years. Unfortunately, they were wrong! Every year the calendar and the seasons drifted one more day apart.

Earth goes round sun once every $365 \frac{1}{4}$ days

28 days pass between each full moon

Caesar's calendar

Julius Caesar asked the best astronomers to fix the problem. Greek-Egyptian expert Sosigenes told Caesar that each year actually lasted 365 1/4 days. He suggested a calendar 365 days long, adding an extra day every four years. The calendar, named "Julian" after Julius Caesar, worked so well that (with a little tweaking 15 centuries later) it has been in use ever since.

Julius Caesar gave his name to the calendar used for centuries.

When Caesar reformed the calendar, harvest time was two months out of step with the seasons.

This Roman calendar is in the form of a stone block. It has the signs of the zodiac on it.

Not quite right

Caesar's changes weren't quite right. Each year actually lasts not 365 days and 6 hours, but 365 days, 5 hours, 49 minutes and 15.974 seconds. So the Julian calendar drifted a day each 128 years. To fix this, Pope Gregory XIII changed the calendar again in 1582. His Gregorian calendar skips a leap year each century – unless the year can be divided by 400. This calendar still isn't quite perfect, but will only be one day wrong by 3500 CE!

ROADS

Viaene omnes vere Romam ducunt?

Stretching away into the distance, a wide road carves a dead-straight line across the landscape. Far beneath the black, shiny tarmac lies an ancient track of crushed stone and gravel. For this route is more than 2000 years old. The Romans built it to carry their powerful armies to the farthest points of their spreading empire.

Rotten roads

Horses' hooves and cartwheels quickly turned roads to dust in summer. Winter rains made them into sticky swamps that swallowed vehicles. Fast, efficient land transport was essential for trade – and later for conquest. So Roman engineers had to find a way to build better roads.

Solid base

Flooding quickly made roads collapse, so Roman road-builders first dug trenches on either side to drain the route. Then they dug out the base of the road, replacing mud with layers of sand, stone and concrete. A top layer of cobble-stones finished the road. Built like this, Roman roads could withstand the heaviest of carts.

A Roman surveyor uses a groma to get the road straight.

Straight surveying

Roman surveyors kept the road straight by lining up the weighted cords of the groma with poles held on the last high-point and the next one.

Veni, vidi, visi.

Marking the route

Digging furrows about 25 m (80 ft) apart helped drain and mark the route. The land between them was cleared.

Roman roads made very fast journeys possible. Tiberius (who later became emperor) set a record when he raced to see his dying brother in 9 BCE. He covered 320 km (200 miles) in a day, wearing out three chariots on the way! Nobody travelled farther in one day until railway lines crossed Europe in the 19th century.

A section of Roman road still in existence. Many Roman roads form the basis of the major highways used today.

Fab foundations

Soldiers building the road dug a trench a metre (40 in) deep and 3-7 m (10-22 ft) wide, plus drainage ditches either side.

Building up the road

Layers of building materials followed: sand, mortar, blocks and slabs, concrete and crushed stone and, to finish off, a final top layer of stones.

Edging the road with heavy kerb stones stopped it spreading in use.

Top layer of tight-fitting stones, gently curved to throw off rain

Concrete with crushed stone

Blocks and slabs in mortar

Trench

Mortar

Sand

WATER SUPPLY

Rome was a city of water. It sprayed from fountains. It splashed without stopping from free public taps in the street. For the price of the smallest coin, Romans could soak in steaming hot water at the public baths. Today this hardly seems surprising. But 2,000 years ago bringing water to Rome was an amazing engineering achievement.

Water woes

Rome's population was huge, and growing. The biggest city in the ancient world, in 50 CE it was the home of a million people. Thirsty people. Some of the water they needed for drinking and washing came from local wells. But they needed much, much more water. And between Rome and the water they needed stood hills and valleys.

Water level had to drop 1 m every 2 km (40 in each mile) to keep it flowing.

To bridge small low points, engineers raised the aqueduct on a wall.

To cross lower valleys, they built an arcade (bridge with arches).

Where possible, the aqueduct snaked round hills, so that the water went very gently downhill.

Tunnels cut through a few hill-tops.

Roman surveyors used instruments like this chorobates to plan the route of aqueducts. When the plumblines (weighted cords) crossed the lines marked on the frame, the bench on top was exactly level. Looking along it allowed surveyors to see how much higher or lower the land ahead was.

Cross-country

To bring more water to Rome, engineers built channels, called aqueducts. To make the water flow, the aqueducts had to slope downwards at a precise angle. To keep this gentle slope constant, they used accurate measuring tools, and made the channels snake around the landscape. They built high bridges to cross valleys, and tunnels to go through hills.

Aqua facts

To carry water across a valley near Lyon, France, Roman engineers made pipes from 10,000 tonnes of lead.

The water that fills Rome's famous Trevi Fountain still comes from the Aqua Virgo, a Roman aqueduct built more than 2000 years ago.

In towns water towers or "castles" divided the supply so that as the level fell, private homes (1) were cut off first, then the baths (2), and public street fountains (3) last of all.

They took water across the deepest gorges with pressurised pipes.

Settling tanks removed dirt and pebbles.

Awash

In 100 CE everyone in Rome had as much water as each person in New York had in 1900.

MECHANICAL ARTILLERY

Fighting a Roman army was a frightening experience. As well as the arrows and spears that all soldiers threw, the Romans used terrifying war machines. Powered by twisted animal gristle they hurled arrows as big as broomsticks, and stone balls the weight of refrigerators. These mighty catapults could hit targets up to 650 m (2130 ft) away, and were more accurate than any archer.

Hair today...

Spring-powered catapults had human hair woven in with the gristle. During the Roman siege of Carthage in 148 BCE, the women of the city cut off their long hair to provide the twisted fibres needed in the torsion spring.

Where's the target?

Earlier war machines, developed in Greece, had two major problems. Their wooden frames were so bulky that they hid the target from view, making aiming difficult; and the bundles of animal gristle that powered them stretched when wet, so they were useless when it rained.

Upper body could be swivelled on its post for aiming.

Metal tubes covered springs

The cheiroballista was a big improvement on earlier examples of mechanical artillery

Sturdy, detachable stand

Smaller, lighter

Roman engineers replaced the wooden frames of smaller catapults with much slimmer metal parts. This created an open frame that warriors could aim just like a modern rifle. Copper or bronze tubes covering the gristle springs made the catapults into all-weather weapons.

Glamour guys

The engineers who designed spring-powered missile throwers were glamorous heroes: they were the rock-stars of the ancient world.

Really big siege engines like the ballista were designed to smash down city walls with stones.

A modern re-enactor loads a small ballista-type weapon.

The ballista

This huge Roman siege engine also utilised twisted-sinew springs. Winching back the arms built up massive tension in order to power shaped-stone projectiles.

Twisted sinew springs

Winch for pulling back rope

Shaped stones of equal weight

SEWERS

We live in a "flush-and-forget" age, but the Romans were not so lucky. So many poor Romans emptied pots-full of sewage from their windows that the city government passed a law to punish those who soaked passers-by. Wealthy Romans escaped justice: those who could afford it had privies (lavatories) linked to a fine sewer system.

Fue! Odor horribilis!

Stinking streets

As Rome grew, it began to stink. Most Romans used pottery jars as lavatories. A smelly cart called at night to remove the contents, which were tipped on fields to make crops grow. But a lot of sewage still ended up on the streets, causing a smelly problem and attracting flies that spread disease.

Dynamic drain

Roman engineers had built a huge gulley, the Cloaca Maxima, in the 7th century BCE to drain marshland so they could build the city's forum (marketplace). A network of sewer pipes carried rainwater into the Cloaca Maxima from city streets. Street sweepers washed street waste into the sewers. Eventually the sewers also drained public lavatories and some private homes.

Privy and kitchen drains in house

Household privies were sometimes flushed with waste water

Public fountain

Street gutter

Sewer pipe

Cloaca Maxima

Fly-tippers
Poor people dumped some of their solid waste on Rome's Esquiline Hill, where they also threw the bodies of animals, and of human relatives they couldn't afford to bury.

Without water-filled U-bends, flies and smells were still a problem in some places.

River Tiber

Da mihi spongiam, sis.

Roman public lavatories were friendly places. Men and women sat side-by-side on marble seats. Instead of paper rolls, there were sponges on sticks, kept clean in a trough of water that ran round the floor.

A wee tax

Laundrymen collected urine to use in washing clothes, and Emperor Vespasian suggested taxing it; when his son Titus complained, the emperor replied, "Why? Does the money smell bad?"

The Cloaca Maxima was 5 metres in diameter. It was beautifully constructed of fitted stone blocks. All the main sewers were big enough to row boats through for inspection

Look out!

This is a blank-verse translation of a poem by the poet Juvenal (late 1st-early 2nd century CE), describing the hazards of going out and about the streets in Rome:

Think of the number of times cracked or broken pots fall out of the windows, of the amount of weight they bring down with a crash onto the street and dent the pavement. Anyone who goes out for dinner without making a will is a fool... you can suffer as many deaths as there are open windows to pass under. So send up a prayer that people will be content with just emptying out their slop bowls!

HEATING

Even sunny Rome had grey, winter days. If the weather got REALLY cold, Romans flocked to the baths. There the fire heating the water also warmed the walls and floor. When Romans invaded northern countries, the colder climate made them shivery and homesick. So they built their homes like their favourite baths in Rome, with underfloor heating called hypocausts.

Nonne aura calida in togam est bona!

That frosty feeling

Rome gets hot in summer. Very hot. So Roman homes were built to be cool. In winter, those who could afford to heated their homes with charcoal stoves, called braziers. They were a lot like today's barbecues. But they did not provide enough heat to keep out the chilly frosts in the northern parts of the Empire.

Surprising fact!

Roman baths heated by hypocausts were noisy places. Roman writer Seneca lived above one, and complained of the screams when slaves plucked their masters' armpit hairs.

Winter warmer

A furnace outside the house supplied hot air for the hypocaust. To allow the hot air to circulate beneath the floor, Roman builders supported it on short columns. Tiles covered the gaps between them. After swirling beneath the floor, the hot air rose through flues (chimneys) running through the walls – so these got hot, too.

This surviving Roman hypocaust clearly shows the bases of the pillars that supported the tiled floor above.

Flues hidden in walls were made by potters in box shapes, and the outside scratched to make plaster stick.

A fancy mosaic floor often covered the tiles.

The Roman hypocaust could keep several rooms warm from a single furnace. No better system was invented until the 18th century.

Tiles cover hypocaust

Furnace

Air circulates through underfloor chamber.

Columns of tiles, bricks or stone support floor.

Slave carries wood to stoke the furnace.

THE DOME

As Roman architects made bigger and grander buildings, they ran into a problem: how to hold the roof up. Adding extra supports was an easy answer. However, in really big buildings the rooms were soon so crowded with columns that you couldn't see to the other side. A better solution was to build an arch that spread out in every direction.

Roof woes

The bigger a building is, the bigger and heavier is its roof. Roman builders knew that roofs made of timber could be light, and span wide, open rooms. But timber roofs were not fireproof. Lintels (stone beams) created fireproof roofs, but in wide rooms they needed supporting columns.

Concrete to the rescue

The answer was to combine two brilliant ideas: concrete (page 6) and arches (page 8). Arches could span great distances, as long as they had strong foundations to stop the top pushing the sides apart. Concrete had great strength, and it could be made light in weight by stirring in foamy, air-filled pumice rock.

By rotating the apex, or top, of an arch (above) and creating from that shape a solid structure, clever Roman engineers came up with another brilliant idea – the dome (right).

Amazing Pantheon

The greatest achievement of the Roman dome-builders was the Pantheon, a vast temple built in 125 CE to honour the many Roman gods. Its huge dome was built so solidly that it still stands today. No building had a circular dome this big until the invention of steel-strengthened concrete more than 1700 years later.

Instead of a keystone, dome has an immensely strong ring of bronze.

Dome weighs some 4500 tonnes (4430 tons).

Central oculus (eye) provides light and ventilation, and reduces weight. Its width is the length of a double-decker bus (more than 8 m/27 ft).

Bubbly pumice stone keeps concrete light at the top.

To reduce weight, dome is much thinner (1.2 m/4 ft at the top than it is at the bottom (6.4 m/21 ft).

Serve you right!

Three tennis courts would fit neatly inside the Pantheon dome, though balls might bounce off the concrete walls.

Sunken panels make dome lighter. They originally had stars painted in them.

Fist-size lumps of extra-hard rock were mixed in to strengthen the thick concrete at the base.

Killjoys

Engineers would not be allowed to build the Pantheon today. Because it contains no steel bars for added strength, modern building inspectors would consider it dangerously unsafe.

GLOSSARY

aim To point a weapon at a TARGET.

amphitheatre Circular or egg-shaped stadium.

arch Curving brick or stone support for a wall or roof, making an opening below.

artillery War engine for hurling things at an enemy.

astronomer Scientist who studies the stars.

cartwheel Hard wooden wheel turning on a cart.

catapult Weapon, powered by a spring, usually used to hurl stones.

cement Powder used to make MORTAR.

centring Temporary frame that supports an ARCH during construction.

chorobates SURVEYING instrument used to pick out points of equal height.

cobblestone Large rounded stone once used to surface roads.

codex Handwritten book.

current A flow, such as the rush of water in a river.

dome Roof shaped like an upside-down bowl.

flue A chimney or hot-air pipe in a wall.

formwork MOULD for concrete used to make a building or part of it.

forum Roman market- and meeting-place.

furrow Deep groove cut in the ground.

gladiator SLAVE trained to fight in combats staged in the AMPHITHEATRE.

grind To crush into a powder.

grindstones A pair of rough round stones, one of which turns, MILLING anything placed between them.

gristle Tough, springy fibre that holds together the bones of an animal.

groma SURVEYING instrument made with four PLUMBLINES hanging from a pair of crossed sticks.

gulley Large underground pipe.

hour-glass A glass bottle with a narrow waist, used like a clock: sand inside takes 60 minutes to fall from the top half to the lower half.

hypocaust Roman hot-air underfloor heating system.

kerb stone Heavy stone placed at the edge of a road to stop the surface from spreading.

keystone Central top block in an ARCH.

laundryman A man who washes clothes and cloth.

lead Soft, grey, easily-shaped metal.

leap year Every fourth year, having 366 days: other years have 365.

lime Powder used in MORTAR which sets into a hard lump when combined with water. Lime is made by heating and crushing LIMESTONE.

limestone Kind of rock used to make LIME.

lintel Strong straight beam of timber or stone used to support the weight of a wall above a door or window.

mill To GRIND; or a building where grinding takes place.

moon phase The shape of that part of the moon lit by the sun, that changes from a circle to a crescent and back each 28 days.

mortar Glue-like paste used to stick together stone or bricks to make walls or roads.

mosaic Pattern on a floor or wall made from tiny, brightly-coloured tiles.

mould Container shaped to enclose a hardening paste such as concrete so that when set, the paste takes the shape of the mould, which is then removed.

munera GLADIATOR battle paid for by a wealthy Roman.

oculus Circular hole in a building, such as at the top of some DOMES.

plumber Worker who shapes lead or joins or makes water pipes.

plumbline String with a weight on one end to keep it hanging straight down.

potter Worker who shapes and bakes clay into pots.

pumice Light frothy kind of stone thrown out by a VOLCANO.

rifle A hand-held gun with a long barrel (firing tube).

rubble Broken lumps of rock.

scroll Roll of writing material such as paper.

settle Falling of solid material such as stones or sand to the bottom of a pool of still liquid.

sewage Liquid and solid waste from the human gut and bladder.

sewer A GULLEY to carry SEWAGE.

slave A captive worker, kept as the property of a free person.

steel Strong metal made mostly of iron.

survey To measure land.

tablet Small, thin, flat piece of hard material.

tamp To ram down hard.

target Something at which a weapon is fired.

tarmac Black tarry material now used to make a road surface smooth, flat and waterproof.

temple Place of worship.

tessera Ticket.

VIP Short for very important person.

volcano Hole in the Earth's solid crust through which melted rock escapes.

COOL STUFF TO SAY IN LATIN

Page 4
Ave!
Hail! (Hello!)

Page 6
Roma in una die non aedificata est.
Rome wasn't built in a day.

Page 8
Stupui videre te hic!
Fancy seeing you here!

Page 10
Da mihi volumem, sis?
Please pass the scroll.

Page 12
Verbera eum!
Thrash him!

Page 14
Medicam turbo!
Spin doctor.

Page 16
Da mihi vinum.
Pass the wine.

Page 18
Viaene omnes vere Romam ducunt?
Do all roads lead to Rome?

Veni, vidi, visi.
I came, I saw, I inspected.

Page 24-25
Fue! Odor horribilis!
Pooh! What a stink!

Da mihi spongiam, sis.
Please pass the sponge on a stick.

Page 26
Nonne aura calida in togam est bona!
That hot air up your toga feels good!

WEBSITES

Construct a Roman aqueduct
http://www.pbs.org/wgbh/nova/lostempires/roman/aqueductjava.html

Roman baths
http://www.pbs.org/wgbh/nova/lostempires/roman/

BBC schools
http://www.bbc.co.uk/schools/romans/

Amphitheatre
http://www.pbs.org/wnet/warriorchallenge/gladiators/interactive_flash.html

Note to parents and teachers:
Every effort has been made by the Publishers to ensure that the websites in this book are suitable for children, that they are of the highest educational value, and that they contain no inappropriate or offensive material. However, because of the nature of the Internet, it is impossible to guarantee that the contents of these sites will not be altered. We strongly advise that Internet access is supervised by a responsible adult.

INDEX